WORK SMARTER NOT HARDER

The *SERVICE THAT SELLS!* Workbook

Foodservice

PEN|COM
INTERNATIONAL

ISBN #1-879239-17-5

PUB-550/1998

Pencom books are available at special discounts when purchased in bulk for premiums and sales promotions, as well as for fund-raising or educational use. Special editions can also be created to specification. For details contact Pencom at the address above.

Contents

Let's Get Started 1
How to Use this Workbook 1

To Sell Is To Serve 3
The Art of the "Soft" Sell 3
Salespeople vs. Order-takers 4

Section One: Product Knowledge 6
    Role Play 9
Action Plan 9

Section Two: Caring Behavior 10
The Seven Steps of Service Excellence 11
Step One: Look at Me 11
Step Two: Smile at Me 11
Step Three: Talk to Me 11
    Role Play 11
Step Four: Listen to Me 12
Step Five: Thank Me 12
Step Six: Remember Me 12
Step Seven: Invite Me Back 12
The Name Game 13
Recognize Your First-Time Guests 13
Clean Up Your Act 14
Action Plan 16

Section Three: Precision Service 17
   1. Initial Contact 17
    Role Play 18
   2. Entrance 18
   3. Greeting and Seating 18
    Role Play 19
   4. Bartender/Cashier 19
   5. Dining Room/Table Condition 19
   6. Buser 19
   7. Server 20
    Role Play 20
   8. Manager 20
   9. Food 20
 10. Restroom 21
 11. Check Presentation 21
 12. Farewell 21
Action Plan 24

Section Four: Sales Performance 25
Pencom Nod 25
    Role Play 26
Use Your Sales Props 27
Use the Right Words 28
Descriptive Adjectives 28
    Role Play 28
Words That Sell 29
The Word "Try" 30
    Role Play 31
The Word "Feature" 31
The Word "Popular" 31
Suggest Mid-Priced Items 31
Always Offer a Choice 31
Suggest Favorites 32
A Shared Sale Beats No Sale 33
Sell within the Zones 33
1. Greeting and Beverage Zone 33
2. Appetizer Zone 34
3. Entree Zone 35
4. Dessert Zone 35
Action Plan 36

Final Action Plan 37
And One Last Thing 40
Pencom International Products 41

Let's Get Started

Work Smarter, Not Harder! The Service That Sells! Workbook for Foodservice differs from other training materials you may have read. The ideas presented are based on the real-world experiences of foodservice employees nationwide. Your colleagues, not your bosses, wrote this workbook. You can be sure its contents are practical and effective — news you can use.

You'll get out of *The Service That Sells! Workbook for Foodservice* exactly what you put into it. Read each page carefully, determine how you can apply the service and sales techniques in your everyday work, and complete the "Put It on Paper" and "It's Your Turn" exercises to the best of your ability. Use role plays — preferably with a manager or trainer — to practice what you've learned.

As a result of your efforts, you'll be able to:

- **Provide better service**
- **Increase your sales**
- **Earn bigger tips**
- **Have more fun at work**

Be open-minded as you complete the workbook. The old way of doing things isn't always the best way. After all, if you always do what you always did, you always get what you always got. *The Service That Sells! Workbook for Foodservice* is the companion of *The Service That Sells! Workbook for Alcohol Beverage Service.* They're powerful in tandem, although either can be used without the other.

How to Use this Workbook

The Service That Sells! Workbook for Foodservice will show you how to give customers what they really want — superior service and a quality dining experience — and help your restaurant achieve what it really needs — higher sales. Along the way, you'll put more cash in your pocket.

The contents are broken down into three key sections — *Caring Behavior, Precision Service* and *Sales Performance* — each inherently connected, each representing an area of opportunity to exceed guests' expectations. Think of them as a "three-legged stool." Without each leg in place, the stool can't stand on its own.

Holding everything together is *Product Knowledge*. You can't care for guests, serve well or sell with consistency if you don't know your menu inside out. You'll be working on your knowledge in Section One before delving into the three legs of *Service That Sells!*

While it's possible to finish the entire workbook in one sitting, it's better to spread it out over four or five days, spending the time to read the introductory material and tackle one section at a time. Ask your manager what time line he or she wants you to follow.

 Be sure to fill out the Action Step at the end of each section. You'll be asked to transfer the best ideas to a Final Action Plan, which will serve as a daily reminder of how you're going to get the most out of completing *Work Smarter, Not Harder! The Service That Sells! Workbook for Foodservice.*

To Sell Is To Serve

A lot of servers, hosts and hostesses won't deny the importance of providing quality customer service, but when asked to sell, they become unglued. "Don't make me do it!" they cry. "Not the S-word. I'll serve all you want, but I don't want to sell!"

Those uncomfortable with selling often feel that way because they dread the possibility of rejection when suggesting menu items to guests. Others shy away from selling simply because they don't know *how* to sell.

Truth is, you can serve all you want, but if you're not selling anything, you're out of business. Consider the story of famed department store founder Marshall Field, who once vowed to go an entire year without buying anything that wasn't sold to him. He claimed he saved $45,000!

In the restaurant business, sales and service go hand in hand. The best way to build rapport with guests is to talk to them. The best thing to talk about is food and beverage — that's why they're there. And the best way to get guests to buy what they've come in for is to sell it to them. Anyone can be an "order-taker." It requires service to sell.

The Art of the "Soft" Sell

Suggestive selling — or soft selling — isn't about bombarding guests with high-priced suggestions. It's asking what they're in the mood for, describing what's good on the menu, and helping them make selections that enhance their dining experience.

Soft selling involves recommending, not *pushing*, specific extras, appetizers, sides, desserts and beverages. It shows guests they're worth your time. It's perceived as attentive service.

You have everything to gain from soft selling (improved sales, tips and service) and little to lose (the guest may say "no thanks"). But in case you're still not convinced, let's look at the difference between salespeople and order-takers.

Salespeople vs. Order-takers

In any restaurant, there are two — and only two — kinds of wait staff:

- Order-takers
- Service-oriented salespeople

Order-takers are walking, talking vending machines. They work harder — *not* smarter — and spend so much time "in the weeds" that even mediocre service is next to impossible. Service-oriented sales-people, on the other hand, serve better and sell more, smiling as they go, controlling the pace and flow of their sections, saving steps, making guests happy and earning bigger tips.

Put it on PAPER

Can you tell the difference between an order-taker and a salesperson? Put an "OT" in the blank below if the phrase describes an order-taker, an "SP" if it describes a salesperson.

_____ *Serves* customers.

_____ Waits tables.

_____ Makes menu suggestions with every guest.

_____ Thinks selling is pushy.

_____ Recommends daily food and drink specials.

_____ Makes small talk with guests to try to get to know them.

_____ Says: "If my customers want it, they'll ask for it."

_____ Recognizes a guest having trouble making a decision and offers guidance.

_____ Is going to get a "real job" someday.

_____ Always suggests appetizers to start and recommends personal favorites.

It's easy to spot salespeople — not only in the way they serve guests, but also in the amount of tips they take home. Let's compare the guest checks of an order-taker and a salesperson, both serving a party of four:

Order-Taker's Tab	
2 diet colas (small)	2.00
2 waters	0
0 appetizers	0
0 side orders	0
1 Grilled Chicken Pasta	8.95
Fajitas for two	10.95
1 cheeseburger	5.95
4 coffees	4.00
desserts	0
Total	$31.85
15% Tip	**$4.78**

Salesperson's Tab	
2 diet colas (large)	3.00
2 flavored iced teas	3.00
1 potato skins	4.95
1 side of sour cream	.75
1 Grilled Chicken Pasta	8.95
Fajitas for two	10.95
1 cheeseburger with bacon	6.70
4 cappuccinos	10.00
2 desserts (shared by all four)	6.00
Total	$54.30
15% Tip	**$8.15**

The bottom line — an $8.15 tip for the salesperson, only $4.78 for the order-taker, a difference of $3.37.

You don't have to sell all the items mentioned to make more money. If you could boost your sales a mere $1 per person — the price of a cup of coffee — you'd take home anywhere from $3,700 to $6,500 in higher tips this year alone, depending on the number of guests you serve. All without working one more minute!

The better you serve, the more you sell. The more you sell, the better you serve. Is this a great concept or what?

Now that you can tell the difference between a salesperson and an order-taker, let's fine tune your product knowledge.

Section One: Product Knowledge

Picture this: You walk into a showroom looking to buy a new mountain bike. You spot a sleek, fire-engine-red model as a salesperson approaches. The conversation goes like this:

Salesperson: "Nice bike, huh?"

You: "Sure is. Does it come in any other colors?"

Salesperson: "Gee, I'm not sure."

You: "Are all these features standard or extra?"

Salesperson: "That's a good question. Let me check."

You: "What's the warranty on it?"

Salesperson: "Does it say there on the tag? I'll go find out."

Sounds like this salesperson is one taco short of a combo platter. Are you going to buy the bike? Not likely, because the salesperson is clueless about the product.

What about you? When guests ask about menu items served in your restaurant, can you answer their questions? If not, you'd better study the menu, getting to know each item in terms of its basic *ingredients* and, where applicable, the *Four P's*:

- Portion
- Preparation
- Presentation
- Price

Let's take a look at the P's in action. Write your favorite entree in the space below, then answer the questions.

My favorite entree:

_____

What are the ingredients?

_____

How big is the portion? (weight or size)

_____

How is it prepared? (fried, baked, broiled, grilled, etc.)

_____

How is it presented? (garnishes)

_____

What's the price?

_____

What would you suggestively sell with it?

_____

You should be well versed in describing the soups, salads, appetizers, entrees, desserts, beverages and specialty items available in your restaurant. If you're a trainee, try to work a shift as a food runner, which will let you see a variety of menu items up close.

Also take the time to know every menu item in terms of features (What is it?) and benefits (What will it do for the guest?). Take an appetizer of stuffed potato skins, for example.

Features:
- You get six large potato skins.
- They're stuffed with cheese, chives and bacon bits.
- They're only $5.95.

Benefits:
- It's a good value for the amount you get.
- There are plenty for two, but enough for four to share.
- They take only 3-5 minutes to prepare.

Reciting features and benefits for guests increases sales of the items you're suggesting. In the spaces below, list the best-sellers at your restaurant under each category in the far left column. Describe their features in the middle column and their benefits in the right column.

The Best Selling...	Features	Benefits
Appetizer		
_____	_____	_____
	_____	_____
	_____	_____
	_____	_____
Entree		
_____	_____	_____
	_____	_____
	_____	_____
	_____	_____
Dessert		
_____	_____	_____
	_____	_____
	_____	_____
	_____	_____

After guests ask "What is that?" or "How is it made?" they'll usually want to know: "How is it?" That's when a skilled server endorses the product to make guests feel good about their purchasing decision. Sample endorsements:

"It's really good."

"It's my favorite."

"It's really popular."

"I just had a sample before the shift. It's great!"

A guest asks about an entree on the menu that you, for whatever reason, haven't tried. Write how you'd respond in the space below:

_____

_____

_____

NOTE: Be prepared to role play this scenario with your manager or trainer.

In the previous scenario, the last thing you want to tell guests is: "I'm not sure. I've never had it." Instead, display confidence in what you're selling. Start with an endorsement: *"You're going to love it."* Then go right into a mouth-watering description of the product, based on your knowledge and perhaps experience serving it to other guests.

There are many ways you can put to work what you've just learned about product knowledge. But, for now, determine the three best ideas you picked up in this section and write them below.

The Three Best Ideas:

1. _____

2. _____

3. _____

At the end of *The Service That Sells! Workbook for Foodservice*, you'll be transferring these ideas to a Final Action Plan, which outlines your time line and game plan for improving your sales and service delivery with the strategies that work best for you.

Section Two: Caring Behavior

At some point in your career, you've probably heard — or maybe even believed — that in order to be successful, all you have to do is maintain a positive attitude. Well, think again. It's not enough to work with a positive attitude if it doesn't result in *behavior* that gets results.

In the list below, compare each point in the attitude column with each point in the behavior column, then circle the one that seems easier to do.

Attitude	Behavior
Have a positive attitude	Smile
Care for your customers	Open doors for guests
Take pride in your job	Wear a clean uniform and apron
Think like a salesperson	Suggest appetizers and desserts to every guest

You should have circled all the items in the "Behavior" column. Sure, it's important to have a good attitude, but the skills associated with service excellence are behavioral in nature. Say you want to drop a few pounds. If your *attitude* is that you're on a diet but your *behavior* leads you to six chocolate donuts for breakfast ... well, we'll see you at Jenny Craig®.

The next strategies form the basis of *Caring Behavior*, the first leg of *Service That Sells!* To truly care for guests is to go out of your way to make them feel important, doing whatever it takes to ensure their dining experience exceeds expectations. It begins with the "Seven Steps of Service Excellence."

The Seven Steps of Service Excellence

Step One: Look at Me

Always make friendly eye contact when greeting guests or acknowledging those waiting for a table. Doing so recognizes their importance and makes them feel comfortable. Avoiding eye contact signals distrust and distaste.

Step Two: Smile at Me

Studies show that people judge others within 30 seconds of meeting them. You can imagine what happens if you greet a guest with a frown ("I'm bummed"), a frantic look ("I'm swamped") or a disinterested look ("You're a bother").

Offering a smile shows you care and that you're going to provide great service. Never lose your show-biz face in front of guests. By the way, you deliver service over the phone, too. Smiling makes your phone voice sound friendlier.

Step Three: Talk to Me

You know, of course, that you should talk to your guests. But what about? Many of them you've never met. Here are topics — positive *hot buttons* — they'll warm to.

- The menu (*"Have you ever tried our famous tortilla soup?"*)
- Profession (*"What do you do?"*)
- Sports (*"How about those Sox?"*)
- Appearance (*"Nice tie!"*)
- Hometown (*"Where are you from?"*)

 The use of hot buttons is an important component of "Table Talk," which is the practice of building rapport with guests and creating service and sales opportunities through friendly conversation. In the space below, write what you could say to a family of four — mom, dad and two kids — to break the ice.

_____

_____

_____

NOTE: Be prepared to role play this scenario with your manager or trainer.

Step Four: Listen to Me

Just as important as talking to guests is *listening* to what they have to say. There are dozens of hidden service and sales opportunities with every guest. All you need to do is listen.

Step Five: Thank Me

Guests like to know their business is appreciated. So thank them. They'll show their gratitude with gratuities.

In the space below, write what you'd say to guests as they're paying their tabs.

_____

_____

_____

Step Six: Remember Me

Customers are people, not a bunch of table numbers coming in and out of your doors. Remembering your regulars, by name, is a little human touch that goes a long way.

In the spaces below, write the names of three regulars who patronize your restaurant.

_____

_____

_____

Step Seven: Invite Me Back

And offer a good reason: *"You'll have to come back and see us for breakfast. Our buttermilk pancakes are delicious."*

The Name Game

One of the most important things you can do to provide *Caring Behavior* is to learn and use guests' names whenever possible. It's what turns newcomers into regulars. Here are ways to help you remember:

- Introduce yourself, then ask who they are. *("Hello, I'm Erica. And you are...?")*
- Repeat their name aloud as soon as possible. *("So, Greg, can I get you something to drink to start?")*
- Repeat their name silently three times, but don't move your lips.
- Use the name frequently *("Have you had a chance to look over the menu, Greg?")*.
- Ask what they do, then associate their names with their occupations.
- Use credit cards to learn guests' names *("Here's your charge slip, Mr. Jones. Come back and see us!")*.

How good is your memory? Look at the people in the five pictures below and memorize their names. You'll be tested later on.

Elmo	*Mr. Walker*	*Ms. Kelminson*	*Alice*	*William*

Recognize Your First-Time Guests

Wouldn't it be great if you knew which guests were visiting your restaurant for the first time? That way you could describe the menu in a little more detail and dial up your *Caring Behavior* a notch or two to make their experience more enjoyable.

Well, it's easy to find out if you ask the right question. Don't say, "Have you ever been here before?" If they have, they might be offended. Instead, say, *"You've been here before, haven't you?"*

This greeting will usually generate one of two responses: "Yes, we have" or "No, we haven't." Armed with this key information, you can structure your sales dialogue accordingly. If, for example, they've never been to your restaurant, you could recommend specials of the house that they just have to try.

What are some other things you can do to pamper first-time guests? Try to come up with three ideas and write them in the blanks below.

1. _____

_____

2. _____

_____

3. _____

_____

Make a commitment to put your ideas into practice. If you pamper first-time guests, they're more likely to become regulars, which means full tables and full tip trays for you and your co-workers.

Clean Up Your Act

A lot rides on your appearance. Guests take immediate notice of the way you look, talk and even smell, then form an impression of you – good or bad. After all, you're the one who'll be handling their food.

Take pride in the way you look. Following are some basic guidelines. Check the box next to the areas you usually have under control.

❑ **Keep your uniform and apron clean.**

Stains tend to accumulate on aprons and shirts at the guest's eye level.

❑ **Don't wear too much makeup, perfume or cologne.**

Great service is a better way of getting attention.

❑ **Don't wear too much jewelry.**

It can transfer germs from people to food.

❑ **Don't handle glassware by the rims.**

A key sanitation issue. More germs spread from hands than any other part of the body. Handling glassware is also a component of *Precision Service*, which you'll be learning about in the next section.

❑ **Keep your fingernails free of dirt.**

Guests see your hands up close.

❑ **Try not to run your hands through your hair or touch your mustache (if you have one).**

Especially since you're handling food!

❑ **Make sure your breath is fresh.**

A wise man once said: "Never refuse a breath mint when offered. There may be a reason it was offered!"

The secret of *Caring Behavior* is to view the dining experience through the eyes of guests, treating them not how you'd like to be treated, but how they'd like to be treated. The Seven Steps of Service Excellence, using guests' names, pampering first-timers, maintaining your appearance — these are all ways to show guests you care.

Speaking of guests, let's see how you do in the "name game." Turn back to page 13 if you need help.

_____   _____   _____   _____   _____

There are many ways you can put to work what you've just learned about *Caring Behavior*. But, for now, determine the three best ideas you picked up in this section and write them below.

The Three Best Ideas:

1. _____

2. _____

3. _____

At the end of *The Service That Sells! Workbook for Foodservice*, you'll be transferring these ideas to a Final Action Plan, which outlines your time line and game plan for improving your sales and service delivery with the strategies that work best for you.

Section Three: Precision Service

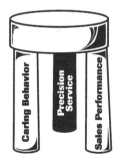

Guests appraise your restaurant whenever and wherever they come in contact with you, your co-workers or the operation itself. Identifying and properly managing your responsibilities at these "Customer Contact Points" — also known as the "Cycle of Service"— will help you produce your share of positive impressions.

The elements of *Caring Behavior* discussed in the previous section will comfort and possibly even delight guests, but they'll lose confidence fast if your service delivery ever gets sloppy. Were you able to greet the table within a minute? Did you get the orders right? How was the pace and flow of meal? Did you reconcile the check quickly?

What you're striving for is *Precision Service*. It's the kind of service that generally goes unnoticed by guests because you and other staff members who visited the table have handled everything, from "hello" to "come back and see us," without a hitch.

The following Customer Contact Points are based on the chronological experience guests would have visiting a typical restaurant. Your contact points may be different or nearly identical. Read each one carefully, determining your role at each point in the Cycle of Service and how to execute it seamlessly.

1. Initial Contact

First impressions are lasting. The initial contact usually occurs over the phone. A guest calling to get directions, for example, should be greeted with a pleasant voice, and given prompt, accurate instructions and a rundown of upcoming promotions.

Our suggestion? Smile when you talk on the phone. You sound friendlier. And don't abandon guests on hold.

Other questions guests might ask:

- Can you tell me about your menu?
- Can I make a reservation?
- What's today's lunch special?
- Which credit cards do you accept?

A guest calls in and asks for directions from the airport. In the space below, write what you'd say.

_____

_____

_____

NOTE: *Be prepared to role play this scenario with your manager or trainer.*

2. Entrance

Imagine yourself entering *your* establishment. How does it look?

Is there trash or debris outside on the way to the front door? Is there an exterior light bulb burned out? Are there cigarette butts, toothpick wrappers, dirty napkins or other litter scattered about?

Pick them up before guests see them. If they come across dirt or debris in a public area, they naturally start doubting the cleanliness of the kitchen.

3. Greeting and Seating

The first employee guests often meet is the host, hostess or greeter. Is that person hiding behind the stand or opening the door for guests as they enter, smiling, welcoming them, learning and using their names?

If you're a greeter, you should never wait for guests to approach. Go to them, anticipating their arrival. Be ready at the door with a cheerful smile and a supply of menus. Make eye contact and use a greeting that suits the guests. They'll appreciate the individual attention.

Whoever seats the guests should pull out chairs, then open and present a menu to each person. It's beneficial to make specific food and beverage recommendations at this point, planting the seed for future sales.

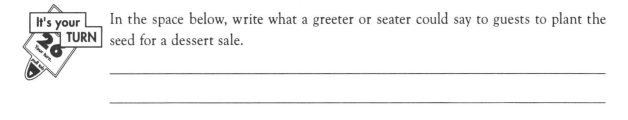

In the space below, write what a greeter or seater could say to guests to plant the seed for a dessert sale.

_____

_____

_____

NOTE: Be prepared to role play this scenario with your manager or trainer.

4. Bartender/Cashier

Bartenders (if your restaurant has a bar) should quickly acknowledge guests with a smile, instead of deciding to wash those dozen glasses first. They must know all the beer, wine and cocktail selections, recognize opportunities to upgrade orders and suggest appropriate food.

Cashiers (if your restaurant has them) should make eye contact, smile and ask departing guests if they've enjoyed their meal. It's best to avoid the question "How was everything?" It tends to come off sounding routine and insincere. A quick glance at the guest check would lead to a better approach: "How was your Southwestern Skillet?"

5. Dining Room/Table Condition

Tabletops and chairs should be wiped down and dried thoroughly. Don't you just hate to sit at a table and discover your hand resting in a mystery substance that some careless server or buser had failed to clean? Crusted stains, sticky salt shakers and dust don't inspire return visits.

Make sure menus, table tents and other props are free of spots and stains, and in good shape. The table should be set with precision and consistency from one table to the next. Look at the surrounding area, too. Is the floor clean or covered with bread crumbs? Guests should never be seated until the table is ready to go.

6. Buser

Busers or service assistants should smile and be friendly. If asked for directions to the nearest bathroom or telephone, they should respond cordially, not just jerk their thumbs in the general direction. And they should never leave the dining room or kitchen empty-handed. Full hands in, full hands out.

7. Server

As you've learned throughout this workbook, servers should see themselves as service-oriented salespeople, not order-takers. You can spot order-takers a mile away just by the manner in which they greet their guests: "Kelp you?" or "Ready?"

As a salesperson, it's your job to *guide* guests through the menu, suggesting items as you go. You should also try to find out a little something about your guests — where they're from, where they work — and, most important, learn, remember and use guests' names.

 In the space below, describe how you'd go about learning guests' names.

_____

_____

_____

NOTE: *Be prepared to role play this scenario with your manager or trainer.*

8. Manager

Managers are salespeople, too. They should recommend specific drinks or food, point out promotions and featured items and survey as much action in the restaurant as possible. They should be *visible* to servers and customers, touching every table, seeking out a stranger.

9. Food

Check back within two bites to make sure the food suits each guest. While you're at it, scan the table for condiments needed — mustard, mayo, a knife, more napkins, etc. — *before* the guest has to ask.

If someone sends back food he or she ordered, for whatever reason, ask any others at the table if you can take their food, too, keeping it hot until the mistake has been resolved. That way everyone can eat together. Your guests will see that you care about their experience and that you're trying to make the best of the situation.

If it's okay with management, follow the "service resolution plus one" approach. Don't charge the guest for the dish that replaced the unsuitable one and throw in a free dessert or perhaps a certificate that can be used the next time the guest comes in.

10. Restroom

Why do you need to keep the restrooms clean? Because it's the sign of a clean restaurant, and in a clean restaurant, people buy more. It's that simple.

It's difficult to suggest and sell a dessert to guests who have just visited a filthy bathroom after enjoying their entrees. Even if it's not your job, help keep the restroom in check, wiping water off the sink tops, restocking supplies, picking up paper and keeping the area tidy whenever you're in there.

11. Check Presentation

Check presentation, during which you present the bill and thank guests for their patronage, may be the most important Customer Contact Point. Why? Because you can handle the previous 10 perfectly, then blow it big time by taking too long to deliver the tab or — worse — taking too long to reconcile it and bring back the guest's change or credit card slip to sign.

Don't put the check down, then disappear into some remote sidework area. Remember: Check down? Check back! After all, guests are deciding your tip at this point.

12. Farewell

This is the critical final step of internal marketing. The effective farewell has two objectives: appreciating the guests on this visit and inviting them back for a return visit.

Example: *"Thanks, Mr. Johnson, Ms. Grant. Come back and see us Friday night for all-you-can-eat ribs."* They'll smile as they walk out, and the guests coming in will notice those smiles and look forward to their experience.

As a review, fill in the Cycle of Service below. You can use the steps already discussed or add ones that seem more appropriate to your restaurant.

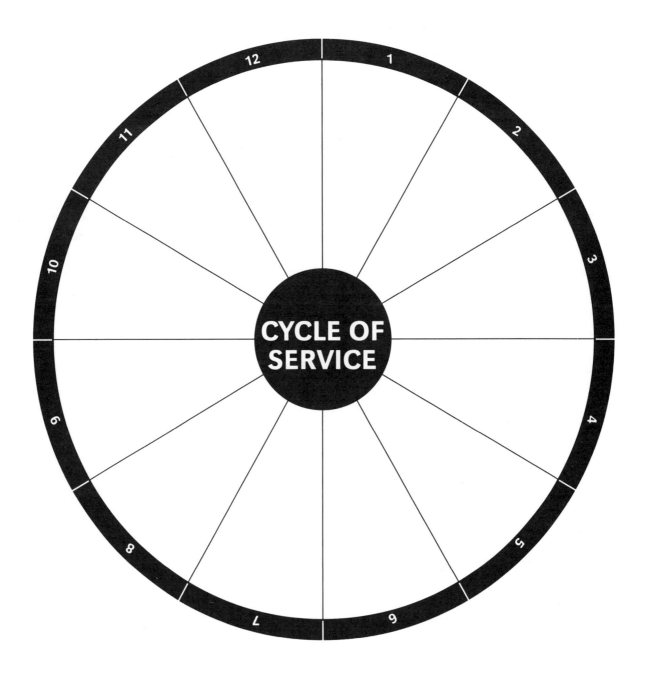

Now that you've determined the differences or similarities between your Cycle of Service and our version, let's examine the behavior that leads to service excellence. What would you have to do in each of the following Customer Contact Points to ensure a great experience for your guests?

Initial Contact – How should you sound on the phone?

_____

_____

Entrance – What can you do to help tidy up the entrance?

_____

_____

Greeting and Seating – How can the greeter plant the seed for future sales?

_____

_____

Bartender/Cashier – If your restaurant has a bar, how can the bartender make "regulars" out of "strangers?"

_____

_____

Dining Room/Table Condition – What should you wipe down when cleaning a table?

_____

_____

Buser – How should the bus staff direct guests to the restroom?

_____

_____

Server – How can you be a salesperson rather than an order-taker?

_____

_____

Manager – What should managers do to be visible to guests?

_____

_____

Food – How soon should you check back on food you've served?

_____

_____

Restroom – What is your role in keeping the restroom clean?

_____

_____

Check Presentation – What should you do after you've presented the check?

_____

_____

Farewell – How can you make sure guests leave happy?

_____

_____

There are many ways you can put to work what you've just learned about *Precision Service*. But, for now, determine the three best ideas you picked up in this section and write them below.

The Three Best Ideas:

1. _____

2. _____

3. _____

At the end of *The Service That Sells! Workbook for Foodservice*, you'll be transferring these ideas to a Final Action Plan, which outlines your time line and game plan for improving your sales and service delivery with the strategies that work best for you.

Section Four: Sales Performance

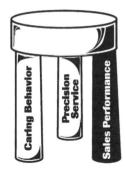

So, you think you're on a roll. You've breezed through the previous sections of this workbook without a hitch. Well, sharpen your pencil and put on your thinking cap — it's time for some *Sales Performance*, the third and final leg of *Service That Sells!*

As you'll recall, the first leg, *Caring Behavior*, is all about making each guest feel important as well as confident in your product knowledge and product wisdom. The second leg, *Precision Service*, refers to the seamless execution of the fundamentals — getting the order right, checking back on food quality within two bites, timing, etc. In short, it's giving guests *what* they want *when* they want it *before* they have to ask.

Sales Performance, equally as important as the other legs, means selling more product, plain and simple, but doing it in a way that demonstrates your commitment to service and enhances guests' dining experiences. You'll be well on your way to success once you equip yourself with the proper sales tools.

Pencom Nod

Forget about your dog. The Pencom Nod is your best friend. And it's easy to master. All you have to do is smile and slowly nod your head up and down as you recommend menu items.

It's amazing how this subtle form of body language coaxes guests into agreeing with your suggestions. Here's the Pencom Nod at work.

Example 1

> Guest: "I'll have a cheeseburger."
>
> Server: (nodding) *"Would you like to try bacon or mushrooms on that?"*
>
> Guest: "Sure, why not?"

Cha-ching! A bigger tip *and* a better tasting burger.

Example 2

> Guest: "What kind of pie do you have today?"
>
> Server: "Cherry, apple and peach."
>
> Guest: "I'll have a slice of peach."
>
> Server: (nodding) *"Would you like that à la mode?"*
>
> Guest: "Yes, that sounds good."

Cha-ching! A bigger tip *and* a happier guest.

Example 3

> You: *(to another server, nodding)* "Would you like to work for me Sunday night?"
>
> Other server: "Oh, sure ... I guess."
>
> You: "Cool."

Wait a minute. If the Pencom Nod is so great, why don't servers all over the world move their head when trying to sell? Fact is, servers *do* move their heads, but too often it's *sideways* instead of up and down, which can trigger a negative response. Many also tend to phrase menu suggestions in the worst possible way. Listen:

> *"You don't want any appetizers, do you?"*
>
> *"You didn't save room for dessert, did you?"*

Heck, no. Not when the question is put *that* way. Here's a better way:

> *"How about some of our* (nodding) *world-famous onion rings or clam chowder to start off with?"*

Sounds better, doesn't it?

 In the space below, name three specific menu items you could sell using the Pencom Nod. While you're at it, write how you'd phrase each suggestion.

Item	Suggestion
1. _____	_____
2. _____	_____
3. _____	_____

NOTE: Be ready to role play the Pencom Nod with your manager or trainer.

The Pencom Nod takes a little practice before it becomes second nature, but once you have it down you'll see your sales go up and up. Many of the next sales strategies incorporate this simple, but powerful, tool.

Use Your Sales Props

The restaurant business is show business, and you should never go on stage without your sales props. If you don't use them, you'll lose out on many sales — and tip — opportunities. Examples of sales props include:

- Table tents
- Appetizer lists
- Menus
- Dessert trays
- Reader boards

Use your sales props when recommending specific menu items. If guests ask about your appetizers, for example, point out a table tent or the list on the menu, reinforcing what you *say* with what they *see*.

Be sure to use your props correctly. Table tents, menus, reader boards and the like should be clean and in good shape, not frayed or torn. Always open the menu when you hand it to guests, highlighting areas of interest.

The food itself can also be used as props. Parade an eye-appealing appetizer by adjacent customers as you deliver it to your table. If you're suggesting an entree to one group, point out guests who are enjoying the dish nearby. If your restaurant has a dessert tray, show it to every guest.

List three sales props you can use in your restaurant:

1. _____

2. _____

3. _____

As the saying goes: "Tools left in the toolbox never built anything." Use your sales props without fail. You'll improve your check averages, and guests will appreciate the extra attention you've shown.

Use the Right Words

In the restaurant business, there are "right" words that can be used to comfort guests and put them in a buying mood. Then there are the "wrong" words that turn guests off like a light switch. Let's look at the right words you should use when suggestive selling and providing top-drawer service.

Descriptive Adjectives

You can't bring out every menu item to show guests what it looks like. That's why using descriptive adjectives — words that create a clear and mouth-watering picture in the minds of guests — is so important. Consider how these servers describe the following entree:

Server A: *"The seafood gumbo casserole has a bunch of fish in it and it's baked in a casserole. People seem to like it."*

Server B: *"The seafood gumbo casserole is one of our most popular entrees. It's six ounces of fresh Florida grouper, stone crab and fresh bay scallops. It's sautéed in white wine, with snow peas, mild peppers and a basil-garlic cream sauce, and baked in a casserole dish with Cajun spices. It comes with a garden salad for only $10.95."*

It's easy to see and hear which server used the right words.

A guest asks about your restaurant's most popular dish. Write it in the space below, then describe it using the right descriptive words.

Dish: _____

The Right Words

_____

_____

_____

NOTE: Be ready to role play this scenario with your manager.

Words That Sell

Here's a list of descriptive words and phrases you can use to make food sound more appealing.

Lightly breaded	Stuffed
Overflowing	Bubbly, melted cheese
Really popular	Fun to share
Spicy, not hot	Fresh daily
Heaping	Extra size
Dip and eat	Super size
Piping hot	Fresh
Unique	Award-winning
Top choice	Center cut
Sautéed	Jumbo stuffed
Seared	Golden brown
Properly aged	Marinated
Honey baked	Jet fresh
Char-broiled	Garden-fresh
Natural	Chilled
New	Famous
Original recipe	Original
Favorite	Savory
Poached	Broasted
Plenty for one, but enough to share	Be sure to save room for ...
Our guests love it	Traditional recipe
Steamed in beer	Brushed in lemon
One-of-a-kind taste	Two-handed
So fresh it slept in the ocean last night	Sold out, not "ran out"

Using the previous list or making up your own, write some descriptive words you'll start using today to put more cash in your pocket.

Appetizers

_____   _____

_____   _____

Desserts

_____   _____

_____   _____

Entrees

_____   _____

_____   _____

The Word "Try"

When suggesting side orders or extras, use the word "try" to let guests know it's going to cost a little more, but it will make the food taste better. Don't forget to use the Pencom Nod. For example:

> Guest: "We'll have the seafood pasta."
>
> Server: (nodding) "Would you like to try some cheese breadsticks to start?"
>
> Guest: "Sure!"

Or:

> Guest: "I'll have the Spanish omelet."
>
> Server: "Would you like to try some sliced avocado on that?"
>
> Guest: "Is it extra?"
>
> Server: "Yes, 75¢, but it makes it taste so much better."
>
> Guest: "Okay."

A guest orders a dessert that could be served à la mode. In the space below, write the dialogue you'd use to sell an add-on of ice cream.

_____

_____

_____

NOTE: *Be ready to role play this scenario with your manager or trainer.*

The Word "Feature"

Doing so is especially helpful when describing appetizers and desserts. For instance: *"Our Three-Layer Mud Pie is the **featured** dessert this evening"* or *"We're **featuring** homemade onion rings tonight for only $2.50."* You can use the word "featured" even if the item isn't discounted. It makes whatever you're suggesting sound special and value-oriented.

The Word "Popular"

Guests often need reassurance when ordering something they haven't had before. Using the word "popular" will put them at ease. Example:

> *Guest:* "How's the chowder?"
>
> *Server:* "It's really popular, the best in town."
>
> *Guest:* "Sounds great!"

Suggest Mid-Priced Items

You gain credibility with guests by recommending popular items and not necessarily the most expensive ones on the menu. Your goal should be to do whatever it takes to enhance the dining experience, not create "sticker shock" by overselling customers. When you serve well, the sales will take care of themselves.

Always Offer a Choice

You may think you work in a restaurant. Truth is, however, you work in retail, selling merchandise the way it's done in a department store. You're a commissioned salesperson for all the "departments" on your menu, including the appetizer department, dessert department and even fresh juice department.

Shoppers, whether they're looking for clothes or something to eat, want choices. In a department store, they can see and handle those choices before deciding to buy. But in a restaurant, all they have to go on are words on a menu or previous experiences. So it's up to you to give guests an "overview" — to suggest at least *two* choices and describe them in mouth-watering detail.

Why two? Let's say you're serving a four-top and recommend only the cheesecake for dessert. The chocolate lovers in the group may not order anything. If you suggest only the chocolate brownie, the cheesecake or pie lovers may lose interest.

Desserts are only part of the picture. If you're suggesting appetizers, don't say: "Did you want an appetizer to start?" It isn't specific and doesn't offer any choices. Try dialogue like this: *"Can I bring you an appetizer to start? The three-cheese quesadillas and stuffed jalapeños are popular and our homemade soup today is beef vegetable."*

See — and hear — the difference?

Suggest Favorites

Your endorsement carries a lot of clout. For instance, you might say: *"Make sure you save room for one of our great desserts. The apple pie is my favorite, but the bread pudding is a close second."*

When a guest asks "What's good today?" describe the specials, and if you've tried one that you especially like, remember to endorse it: *"I tried the chicken vegetable soup before my shift and it's really good."*

Put it on PAPER — What are your favorite items served in your restaurant? Write the top two under the following categories.

Entrees

_____

_____

Soups and Salads

_____

_____

Appetizers

_____

_____

Desserts

_____

_____

A Shared Sale Beats No Sale

When suggesting appetizers and desserts, have you ever noticed that some guests never quite say yes or no? They may mumble that they're "kind of full" or "not sure." Indecisive guests want guidance. Who better to offer direction than you?

If you suggest dessert and a party of two or more hesitates, never say: "I'll give you a few more minutes" and then leave the table. Instead, suggest they share, using this dialogue: "You know, all of our desserts come with multiple forks!" The same strategy works well when suggesting appetizers.

Write three items served in your restaurant that can be shared by two or more guests:

1. _____

2. _____

3. _____

Sell within the Zones

"Selling Zones" represent windows of opportunity during the meal to guide guests through the menu. It's all about making helpful and appreciated recommendations.

1. Greeting and Beverage Zone

First and foremost, greet customers quickly. Always have a specific idea of the beverages you're going to suggest, using the Law of Primacy and Recency.

Say what?

All primacy and recency means is that people tend to remember the first and last things you say. It's a trick advertisers have been using for years.

Here's how it works. Just mention the menu item twice when suggesting it to your customers — in general at first, then get more specific at the end. Say you want to increase your specialty coffee sales. This could be your approach:

> "Hello, what can I start you off with to drink? Coffee, a soft drink, an iced tea (nodding)? Tonight we're featuring our cappuccinos and lattes."

Did you notice how the sales dialogue mentioned coffee in general at first, then reinforced it with a specific type last? This psychological tug usually will get guests to consider your suggestion.

If you want to sell more juice, try this:

> *"What can I get you to drink? A glass of juice, a cup of coffee, tea (nodding)? We have fresh-squeezed orange and grapefruit juice."*

Put it on PAPER

Now you try. Say you want to suggest a special Strawberry Iced Tea to guests. In the space below, write what you might say using the Law of Primacy and Recency.

Your sales dialogue: _____

_____

_____

_____

The Greeting and Beverage Zone is also the spot to plant the seed for the appetizer sale: *"While I'm getting your Strawberry Iced Teas, look over our appetizer list. We're famous for our nachos, and the homemade soup is Wisconsin Cheese."*

2. Appetizer Zone

After returning with the beverage order, *assume* your guests want an appetizer. You may hear "no thanks" from a four-top when you suggest something, but that doesn't mean you shouldn't try again with another four-top.

In "assuming the sale," you're confident that not only you can sell, but also your customers want to buy. It's a fact of life that salespeople are in the business of assuming success, not failure. Listen to the assumption used in this dialogue:

> *"Have you had a chance to look over the appetizers? Which can I bring you?"*

If the table declines, you haven't braved rejection for nothing. Those guests might be interested in an appetizer the next time they come in. You've planted the seed now for a sale later.

When making suggestions and assuming the sale, try not to ask questions that can be answered with a yes or no. Example:

1. "Anybody want something to start?"

2. "Would you like an appetizer?"

3. "You don't want to try some guacamole on your nachos, do you?"

Put it on PAPER

Let's re-phrase these three inquiries as open-ended questions. The first two are phrased correctly for you. You fill in the third.

1. "How about our spinach dip or an order of our award-winning onion rings to start?"

2. "The buffalo chicken wings and the calamari are really popular. Which one can I bring you?"

3. _____

While you're in the Appetizer Zone, keep in mind the other sales strategies you've learned. Offer a choice ("*The potato skins and smoked trout are both very good*"), then recommend your favorite ("But my *favorite is the chicken Caesar salad.*")

3. Entree Zone

Describe daily specials and compliment guests on their selections ("*Good choice!*"). Take the order, suggesting sides or extras that go well with the entree. Grilled onions, bacon and mushrooms would enhance a burger, a side of guacamole would suit that burrito.

At some point in the Entree Zone, remind guests to save room for dessert ("*Don't get too filled up. Our Chocolate Decadence Cake is out of this world and our Peach Cobbler is to die for.*")

4. Dessert Zone

You may not know this, but desserts are internationally recognized as the Fifth Food Group. The Dessert Zone includes desserts, coffee, tea, espressos, cappuccinos and other specialty beverages. If possible, use a dessert tray or specialty coffee list.

Always suggest dessert before you mention coffee. Coffee tends to signal the end of the meal. If a guest declines dessert, suggest cappuccinos or lattes ahead of regular or decaf coffee. And don't forget to nod.

Think of a menu item you could recommend in each of the Selling Zones below, then in the spaces provided write the dialogue you'd use:

Greeting and Beverage Zone

_____

_____

Appetizer Zone

_____

_____

Entree Zone

_____

_____

Dessert Zone

_____

_____

When selling within the zones, it's essential that you know what you want to suggest while you're there and what to suggest before you leave, thus "planting the seed" for sales success in the next zone. Stick to your strategy with each table you serve. Your consistency will pay off.

There are many ways you can put to work what you've just learned about *Sales Performance*. But, for now, determine the three best ideas you picked up in this section and write them below.

The Three Best Ideas:

1. _____

2. _____

3. _____

At the end of *The Service That Sells! Workbook for Foodservice*, you'll be transferring these ideas to a Final Action Plan, which outlines your time line and game plan for improving your sales and service delivery with the strategies that work best for you.

In fact, it starts on the next page.

Final Action Plan

The last task in *Work Smarter, Not Harder! The Service That Sells! Workbook for Foodservice* is to figure out how you're going to do what you've just learned to do. The best advice? Just do it.

In the Final Action Plan starting below and continuing on the next three pages, transfer the "Action Steps" you identified at the end of each section — pages 9, 16, 24, 36. You should have 12 total.

Write the "Start Date" you plan to implement each Action Step. A month later return to this Final Action Plan and describe the "30-Day Results" you've experienced. We're sure you'll be pleasantly surprised.

Section One: Product Knowledge

1 Action Step:

Start Date:

30-Day Results:

2 Action Step:

Start Date:

30-Day Results:

3 Action Step:

Start Date:

30-Day Results:

Section Two: Caring Behavior

4 Action Step:

Start Date:

30-Day Results:

5 Action Step:

Start Date:

30-Day Results:

6 Action Step:

Start Date:

30-Day Results:

Section Three: Precision Service

7 Action Step:

Start Date:

30-Day Results:

8 Action Step:

Start Date:

30-Day Results:

9 Action Step:

Start Date:

30-Day Results:

Section Four: Sales Performance

| 10 | Action Step:

Start Date:

30-Day Results:

| 11 | Action Step:

Start Date:

30-Day Results:

| 12 | Action Step:

Start Date:

30-Day Results:

And One Last Thing...

Now that you've completed *Work Smarter, Not Harder! The Service That Sells! Workbook for Foodservice*, it's up to you to put the ideas to work. You have everything to gain — higher sales, bigger tips, better service — and nothing to lose.

Here's how to maximize your results:

- Keep your Final Action Plan where you can refer to it. Make a commitment to put the ideas to use.
- Keep track of how much your tips increase after reading the workbook.
- Re-read the workbook from time to time. You may pick up on something you missed the first time around.

Pencom International Products ... to build your bottom line.

VIDEOS

Service That Sells! The Art of Profitable Hospitality

The 12 Moments of Truth that made *Service That Sells!* an international success have been updated in this new release of our best-selling video. *Caring Behavior, Precision Service* and *Sales Performance* — the three legs of *Service That Sells!* — will show your staff how to manage the guest experience effectively from start to finish. *Full Service version* **$99**; *Family Dining version* **$99**

CheckBusters: The Art of Smart Selling

Raise check averages a minimum of 25 cents per person — or your money back. Fun and fast-paced, *CheckBusters* is loaded with tips and techniques that promote sales while enhancing how guests perceive the quality of service your staff provides. **$149**

CheckBusters Workbooks. Ideal for a comprehensive program and training retention. **25 for $69.95; 50 for $99.95**

Heads Up! Tapping into Craft Beer

More fun than a hoppy pilsner, *Heads Up!* demystifies the endless varieties of craft beer on the market, giving bartenders and servers the knowledge and brewing background they need to sell and serve with the best. **$69**

Pour on the Profits

Teach your staff how to maximize sales and service potential at the bar using "table talk" to break down conversational barriers and "product wisdom" to put guests in a buying mood. **$99**

The "Sell More" Series

Focus your sales training with the "Sell More" series. Perfect for viewing at pre-shift meetings.

Sell More Beer — **$69**

Sell More Wine — **$69**

Sell More Appetizers — **$69**

Sell More Desserts — **$69**

Uncommon Grounds:
Cashing in on the Coffee Craze

Educate servers in the art of selling and serving specialty coffees. *Uncommon Grounds* explores the ins and outs of preparation, product knowledge and promoting add-ons. **$69**

NEWSLETTER

The Service That Sells! Newsletter

Get the edge on your competition for a quarter a day. Service, sales, cost control, leadership, marketing — the management tool you need to run a profitable operation. One-year subscription **$99**, two-year subscription **$149**. Canada **$139** per year. International **$169** per year. Multiple subscription rates available.

BOOKS

Service That Sells!
The Art of Profitable Hospitality

This is it. The best-selling book in foodservice history. More than 300,000 sold. An indispensable resource for restaurant owners, operators and managers committed to profitable hospitality and getting the most out of their employees. *English* or *Spanish* **$16.95**

Quick Service That Sells!

The profit-building approach that made *STS! The Book* a best-seller is adapted to quick service in this must-have resource. Speed, accuracy, quality, value, consistency, service, atmosphere, personalization – *Quick Service That Sells!* shows QSR operators how to excel in these critical moments of truth. **$16.95**

Turn the Tables on Turnover: 52 Ways To Find, Hire and Keep the Best Hospitality Employees

Lower your turnover by bringing on the right employees and giving them plenty of reasons to stay. **$19.95**

Playing Games at Work: 52 Best Incentives, Contests and Rewards

Boost staff morale and productivity with these fun, manageable and results-oriented incentive programs, contributed by readers of the *Service That Sells! Newsletter*. **$19.95**

Pump Up Your Profits: 52 Cost-Saving Ideas To Build Your Bottom Line

Save a bundle in lost revenue this year with tried-and-true measures to widen your profit margins and narrow your wasteful practices. **$19.95**

Pour It On: 52 Ways To Maximize Bar Sales

Make the most of your adult-beverage sales and service with this invaluable behind-the-bar tool. **$19.95**

All for One: 52 Ways To Build a Winning Team

Discover how to choose the right team players, develop team-building skills and unite the entire staff with these strategies. **$19.95**

www.pencominternational.com

Get connected

The Pencom International Website is more than a company snapshot. It's a meeting of the minds, where foodservice operators and manufacturers can:

- Interact in a virtual exchange of ideas
- Take part in hot-button industry polls
- Get Real World Training Solutions

All at the click of a mouse.

Updated weekly, the website delivers free sample pages of the *Service That Sells!* Newsletter, restaurant-tested productivity tools and techniques, exclusive offers for visitors, and links to many other important foodservice sites.

Hop online. Every product in this listing — and many more — can be ordered off the Pencom International Website through a secure line. Save time when you know what you want. Get the solutions you need – when you need them. Visit us today at **www.pencominternational.com.**